SHERMAN PACES

PASSIVE INCOME FREEDOM

The Ultimate Guide to Passive Income, Discover the Blueprint and the Different Strategies on How You Can Earn Consistent Passive Income

Descrierea CIP a Bibliotecii Naționale a României
SHERMAN PACES
   PASSIVE INCOME FREEDOM. The Ultimate Guide to
Passive Income, Discover the Blueprint and the Different
Strategies on How You Can Earn Consistent Passive Income /
Sherman Paces. – Bucharest: Editura My Ebook, 2020
   ISBN

SHERMAN PACES

PASSIVE INCOME FREEDOM

The Ultimate Guide to Passive Income, Discover the Blueprint and the Different Strategies on How You Can Earn Consistent Passive Income

My Ebook Publishing House
Bucharest, 2020

TABLE OF CONTENTS

PASSIVE INCOME

Passive income is a source of revenue you ideally create only once, to bring in fresh batches of income over and over, all on its own. Once optimized, promoted and set up to run, it requires *no further action* to initiate each new "sale", unlike residual recurring income from programs like membership sites, which are often dependent on ongoing services provided, as well as interaction from the owner.

Every marketer should add some form of passive income to his sales funnel, no matter what area he plans to make his primary focus. Not generating passive income is a sad waste of existing sites, materials or opportunities. Not to take advantage of as many streams of income possible from your work is what is famously (or infamously) called "leaving money on the table". But it's a sad waste to present your offer as a one-time, isolated event.

If you are choosing to pass on passive income, you are ignoring a self - renewing treasure chest of ready "extra" cash there for the taking. You have put the hard work into setting up your internet marketing ventures... Why not make the most of your efforts? Make sure you've reaped every last penny, before you move on to a new venture.

Not sure exactly what passive income is – and isn't? Or how to start the ball rolling? This guide will demystify the subject and help you pick and choose your best options, so you can add passive income to your unique internet marketing adventure with confidence.

NO SUCH THING AS TRUE
"AUTOPILOT RICHES"?

The bad news about passive income? The "passive" part is misleading: There is always some focused work at the beginning, which can feel like a lot, to a new marketer.

Sometimes, if you're really new, there is a sharp *learning curve* as you learn to operate the other necessary programs, methods or systems you need for your business. But it's well worth the effort to go that step further to creating passive income from as many sources as possible, because once you've set up your passive income plants, with just a little watering now and then, you really can make steady autopilot profit.

How much – and how *labor intensive* your efforts will have to be – depends on a number of factors...

- **How many sites you set up**. To put it into perspective, if you plant one tomato plant, that little plant might give off a bumper crop of tomatoes to eat at home – but 50 plants would give you enough to sell at a roadside stand. So it is with passive income: The more ventures you have working for you, the more income keeps flooding in.

- **Which particular passive income method you choose**. Some are better than others at producing a high sales or profit yield – but no matter what method you decide on, there are actions you can take to dramatically increase the amount of income your chosen method is capable of generating for you. (And it's important to suit the method and the media to the campaign.)

- **Whether or not you run an affiliate program**. Running an affiliate program is not as daunting as it may sound. Later on, I'll show you an easy way to run an affiliate program with very little work. Affiliates sell your product to their list… and each member in turn may sell it to his or her list… When you stop to think, it makes no sense to sell a product and not have affiliates to multiply those sales with their own lists!

- **Whether or not you are diligent about tracking**. It's no secret that the most lucrative forms of passive income benefit from *regular tracking*. This shouldn't be intimidating: There are many different tracking options, and we will discuss the most common in this report.

- **Whether or not you decide to use paid advertising**. There is no doubt that using PPC (pay per click) advertising such as Google AdWords can significantly boost your passive income results. But is it the best strategy for new marketers?

- **How much you diversify.** The old cliché: "Don't put all your eggs in one basket" is a good one, particularly when it comes to online passive income. But there's a fine line between diversifying, and overwhelming yourself with too many passive income sources in too many places. Which brings us to our next point…

- **How organized you are**. It's crucial to be on top of your passive income empire, aware of what's going on with each "branch" – you can lose serious cash or opportunities by ignoring tracking, presenting offers to the wrong market, or assuming everything's running

11

like clockwork. We're going to discuss solid methods for making sure unnecessary loss doesn't happen to you.

- **How accurately you do your keyword research**. Research is one of the most important areas to "get right" – and even top marketers will tell you it's still "trial and error". But even though we're going to talk about keywords, there's an added level of depth to the subject of knowing your niche that we're about to thoroughly explore.

And, of course, whichever method(s) of online passive income you choose as your income-generating vehicle – you'll need to know how to *drive traffic* to your site.

Before we tackle the vital subject of search engine optimization, there is something even more important you need to do...

BECOME ABSOLUTELY INDISPENSABLE (AND MEMORABLE) TO YOUR MARKET

One of the biggest misconceptions in internet marketing involves the primary research you must do in order to succeed in any niche.

Usually, all we hear about is keywords, keywords, keywords. Well, keywords are important – and we will get to that – but the first thing you must do is **make a strong, personal connection** with every individual in your target market.

Tall order, much?

Not as tall as you might think: There are 2 highly effective ways to achieve this goal – neither of them as touchy-feely nor labor-intensive as I've startled you into suspecting.

1. Find a **great product** to promote and sell. Then go out and find the *exact person* who is *desperate for that product –*

who attaches a value to it much higher than its actual cash price tag ("perceived value")

2. Find a group of people with **an overwhelming need or unsolved problem** – and fill it/solve it.

Either way, your focus should *not* be all about extracting money from your niche market – it should be about *providing everything they need* and *helping each one succeed*. The paradox here is… when you put aside your own needs and focus on the needs of each individual who trusts you enough to subscribe, you **create a value on your name and services** that is a bigger asset than all the initial quick sales in the world.

What you are doing is **playing matchmaker** who brings 2 soul mates – product and person – together. Your message is, "Hey, I know everything you need – and I can give you the things you can't find."

You are the neighbor who rushes in with the vital missing ingredient – right before the dinner party is about to become a disaster! Your message is: "Here it is! I saw you were in trouble, so I rushed over straight away, even before you asked."

If you think of yourself as the person who stops all gaps, provides the Band-Aids and reassurance, builds their confidence and helps them succeed – just like you would your own kids, or sister, or best friend – you'll soon find yourself providing your market with high value offerings automatically.

And – what is more important – they'll think of *you*, that way, too.

Gaining your niche market's trust is the most intangible yet most vital asset anyone hoping to profit from ongoing passive income could ever create.

You don't do it by staying "in your head", detached from their problems. You need to *feel* their problems – by getting to really know them – in order to meet the challenge of becoming a true leader in their eyes.

HOW TO CREATE THE PERFECT MATCH

It helps if you are passionate about the niche you've decided to work – but I've learned from personal experience that *it isn't always necessary* to be so. Sometimes you find a product that's way outside your normal area of interest, but it's got all the hallmarks of success stamped all over it.

If you find one that's a gem like this, you quickly grow genuinely passionate about it – because it's going to make you money, and you're going to get a warm, fuzzy feeling from pleasing the target niche market who perceives your great product as truly perfect!

(If it's truly outside your normal list, that's when you would *quickly create and promote a new mini site for it*, anonymously, because your name at this point would not be an asset.) All that's left to do, before you rush to sign up, is find the market for your wonder product.)

Having an eye for a product – or a niche – or a need – may feel difficult, at first, but it's something that quickly becomes second - nature.

Positioning Doesn't Happen by Accident

There's more to becoming indispensable to your niche than just filling product gaps: you also need to **position** yourself at the top, and **leverage** your competition.

This is not as hard as it sounds. If you're new, you don't have to make a public fanfare of the fact that you're new. If you've done your homework and you're convinced you've got just the product for your niche – go ahead! Let them know you're the person they need to hurry to, in order to get that prized product.

As for your competition, having competition is a good thing. There's truth in the saying: "*If there is competition in a niche, it can make you money.*"

If You Can't Beat Them, Join Them…

Of course, you don't want to focus on too broad a niche, or too big a competitor. But if you can't beat the top "super affiliates", **put them to work for you!**

Of course, you don't position it that way... What you actually do is: You tell the super affiliate you've found the perfect product for her list, and propose a simple JV (joint venture) partnership with her. It doesn't matter how new you are – if you present your proposal professionally and, above all, you have an offer that's highly targeted to her list, she'll be interested! (Top marketers are always hungry for list-pleasing offers.)

3 things that will greatly increase your chance of receiving a "yes" answer from a super affiliate?

1. Offer a **high commission** – if you have no list yourself yet, perhaps even 100% (it's worth it, to add her subscribers to your own list!) Another option is *lifetime cookies*, so she continues to reap recurring income from repeat sales from that customer.

2. If the item is a report or eBook you've created, make sure you allow the super affiliate to **brand** it with her own name and information

3. Keep in mind that super affiliates usually don't waste their time on low ticket items. You're much more likely to receive a "yes" if the sale is worth their while. (How low they'll start is unique to every super affiliate.)

So, to recap, it doesn't really matter whether you started with:

- A great product
- A great niche
- A great long-tailed keyword

Follow the principles laid out above, and you'll rise more quickly through the ranks, gaining visibility – and credibility.

INCREASING YOUR VISIBILITY

Don't forget to use **Social media** to boost your web presence and – far more important – to connect with members of your niche. You can use whichever social media you're most comfortable with: **Facebook, Twitter, MySpace** or **FriendFeed** – it really doesn't matter as long as:

- Your target subscribers will be there

- You're comfortable with using that particular platform

For myself, I like Twitter. It's fast, it's immediate – and people are highly inclined to impulsively click on Twitter links.

You see, what you are actually trying to do with social media is "create a buzz" – get everyone treating you as if you're the hottest thing since Jalapeno peppers. We've already learned that one way to do that is to *position* yourself alongside the niche leaders – which is surprisingly easy to do on a platform like Twitter, where everyone is equal and even celebrities chatter to all and sundry.

Use **Article Marketing** too, of course – you should know the basics of that promotional vehicle, by now. If you don't, it's not rocket science. Write short 500 word articles that would be highly interesting to members of your niche, and submit them to directories like ezinearticles.com – with a strong, well-crafted *resource box* attached.

And it goes without saying that you'd have a blog – perhaps even one set up to showcase or promote a particular product. Perhaps many. (If you're niche blogging, "many" is essential: you won't create significant passive income with one or two blogs.)

SEO AND PASSIVE INCOME

Another asset you will need, if you truly want to grow your passive income efforts to maximum proportions: Effective **Search Engine Optimization.**

Before your stomach starts to knot at the thought of delving into SEO, however, forget any ideas you might have involving complex algorithms, costly subscriptions, an ad budget that breaks your piggybank, clever manipulation of META-data, or hours of time.

SEO is really quite simple, and the only constant that seems to be in play this new decade is another *paradox*: SEO blog post complaints and forum posts all seem to be confirming that the more you attempt to artificially or even just intelligently boost yourself in Google's rankings, the less likely you are, these days, to succeed.

Today, more than ever, writing original content that speaks directly to your target subscriber is essential – but don't confuse original content with "clever" content. This has nothing to do with digging up statistically favorable long tailed keywords – and everything to do with **completely empathizing with your reader** and making him feel you and he are having a satisfying, helpful and enjoyable **conversation**. That's the real meaning of "killer content"!

Yes, by all means research keywords; but keep it simple, and don't waste time trying to be too foxy. Observe a few core rules and focus on writing articles and posts that really do give your readers the candy they've been craving in secret.

Conclude every post with a "call to action", speak *to* them, not *at* them: in short, drive them **naturally** to your squeeze pages and sites.

And my biggest secret? Don't forget to **go for it with everything you've got**.

Never, ever apologize, or cringe away from presenting that offer. As long as you're matching the *perfect product* with the *right person,* they're going to perceive that you did them an enormous, personal favor – and you're headed straight down the right highway towards Successville!

"ONLY MY MOM LOVES MY BLOG":
A CASE STUDY

We've established that, no matter which way you're generating passive income, you need to be seen as *someone with the answers*, who *genuinely cares* about your readers or followers. We've talked about natural, organic SEO. This is primarily the heart of your market position –

But what do you actually do, when it comes to practical keyword research?

Here's a fact:

- You can manipulate the search engine results far less than you used to be able to, even three years ago – and that applies to both "black hat" techniques, or white

Don't let anyone fool you: It really *is* all about the content – more than ever.

For example, a recent post on Problogger, "*Why Nobody Cares About Your Blog*", unleashed a storm of comments

(139 comments; and they're still flooding in at time of writing). The author, David Risley, was speaking of the importance of speaking *to* people, not *at* them. In page after page of answers, 3 common refrains repeated over and over again.

1. An overwhelming number admitted they had **low to no traffic** – many of them after genuinely diligent keyword research, original content, and several months' (even years') work invested

2. Another noticeable, if smaller, segment of this group had **noticeably poor communication skills.** It was no surprise they had a dismal lack of readership.

3. We can disregard this one, for our purposes: (Each commenter was writing a **personal blog just for himself** and wrote to say that he or she didn't care if there was any traffic.)

I checked out several of these blogs, and found some total gems. Of these gems, however, 2 "themes" common to self-admitted "unsuccessful" bloggers emerged:

1. The blogger seems to have made **no attempt other than SEO** to position themselves to their target market – he or she was not linking to social media, did not have high Twitter or Facebook profiles – and were talking about things relating to *their own* needs and experiences, hoping to connect

2. Even though the blogger's content was superb, **the niche he or she had chosen was far too broad**. The chances of people finding them organically, as a result, were microscopically small.

The majority of all commenters were struck by the fact they had slipped into talking "<u>at</u>" their readership, not "*to*" them – and you may be realizing this too. But if you step back even further and zoom out, you'll notice another fact:

Author David Risley is now known as a "leader" to 139 (and rising) more people. It doesn't matter that he's already a six-figure blogger: Before I read that blog post, I did not know his name. (It's entirely possible the remaining 138 didn't, either.)

How did my new awareness of his existence suddenly happen? 4 factors came into play:

1. The ProBlogger owner, Darren Rowse, **Tweeted it on Twitter**

2. The title, "*Why Nobody Cares About Your Blog*", was **irresistible**, and was **talking directly to me**. Even though I'm secure about my blog, it intrigued me (and I admit, created a slight anxiety in the pit of my stomach). I had to check it out.

3. Problogger is an established blogging **community leader**. If it's endorsed by Darren Rowse, I'm more likely to check out a link. And I'm already subscribed to Problogger.

4. David Risley was smart enough to get himself a **guest post** on a community leading blog with a built in "audience".

You can see how all these factors worked together organically: If David Risley's article had been labeled with a boring, generic title like: *"Getting More Traffic To Your Blog"* - chances are, Problogger guest post or not, I would have given it a miss that day, since I was particularly busy. But *"Why Nobody Cares About Your Blog"* was *personal* – it got me in the gut. Even though I hadn't met him yet, David Risley was **speaking directly to me**.

But even with the fantastic title, I would probably never have found David Risley's post, if he had kept it to his own private blog. I simply **wouldn't have known he existed**.

Then again, even as a guest on Darren Rowse's Problogger blog, and even with the post having such a great title, I most likely would have missed it anyway, being really busy – if I hadn't checked **Twitter**, which I do several times a day.

So, to recap, David Risley had several things going for him:

- **Positioning through a JV** (a guest blog spot on Problogger)

- An **intriguing, irresistible headline** that mattered to me, personally

- Strong content that **spoke directly to his listeners**

- A **JV partner** who promoted him (Darren's Tweet)

- **Great SEO** (ProBlogger rank is way up there)

- **Social Media exposure**

You can see why any *one* of these things is powerful – but put them all together in a focused package – and David Risley instantly became "buzzworthy"!

The organic part – based on good solid practices – was *how it all came together* and spoke to a niche that was, in this case, unusually broad – bloggers. Of all shapes, colors and sizes.

That's no mean feat!

You may be asking yourself at this point: "*But what does all this have to do with Passive Income?* Get on with it! Show me how to create it!"

Relax! That's exactly what we're doing, you know. There's a powerful reason I've spent so much time talking about SEO, connection with your niche, market exposure and positioning:

- Without a **thorough, visceral** and **personal grasp** of the way it all inter-relates, your passive income is going to be a dribble instead of a flood.

It would be too easy to give you a succinct list of elements to incorporate. The danger with this standard approach: If you're newer to marketing, you might understand each item on this list clearly while reading it.. but the moment you go to implement it all, you get distracted and confused, and you're not quite sure how to put it into practice. This is what we might call, "the difference between *theory* and *practice*."

You see, it's not enough to know **what** to do – it's not even enough to know **how** to do it. You need to experience and absorb the "**why**".

Take a tip from the page of professional storytellers – the sort that don't read from a book, but really *tell* a story. They get invited to festivals all over the world.

Their trick? When they're learning a story, they tell it until they live it: In other words, they "make it their own".

You too need to take that "why" and "make it your own". A case study can show you the what and the **how** in action – which helps you to grasp the "**why**" on a deeper gut level.

So... Put the good practices we've just seen into play – and we've automatically got serious traffic to drive to all our passive income points! Right?

SIMPLE AFFILIATE SECRETS

Well, not quite – but we're almost there! We just have to throw *one more ingredient* into the mix: Namely, your most important method of passive income growth – *no matter what method you're using* to generate that passive income.

And that is having **your own product and affiliate program**. And (like David Risley) using the joint venture principle to set into motion. (It doesn't matter that his post had nothing to do with driving people to a passive income product: *the principle is the same.*)

Think of it: You're Jane Doe, with a tiny list of 78 people. You set up an affiliate program for your product – either by installing an affiliate manager script, using a shopping cart that allows you to set one up, or even (if you really don't have a clue how to do that, and you're too nervous to try) by putting your product on Clickbank, which automatically sets up an affiliate program for you as part of its service. (For a one-time fee of $50, that's not a bad deal!)

You create resources for your affiliates, downloadable from a private section of your blog that they can easily access by using the log-in password you've set up for them. Resources would include helpful items like snippets of code, banner ads, button ads, PLR, templates, headers… whatever you choose to include, to help them to sell your product!

With your new affiliate program ready and waiting, you contact a **super affiliate** like Rosalind Gardner, and show her the information product you've specifically created for the niche you know she supplies with product recommendations.

You wisely offer her a **great commission rate** (maybe even with **lifetime cookies** – you aren't taking any chances!)

You make sure there is **nothing on your sales page that will kill her interest** on the spot by accidentally diverting credit for the sale away from her.

You offer to **do all the work for her** – you know how busy she is – and provide her with *a direct download link* to your product and *her own personal affiliate link* on the spot, so she doesn't even have to bother signing up.

Impressed with your sales page and professionalism, she checks out your product, and **seeing that it will indeed please**

her list (and **generate sales**!) - she agrees to **JV** with you by **writing a review**.

Rosalind Gardner's list is massive – she's the mother of all super affiliates! You are suddenly flooded with sales, and you **capture each person** who buys straight to your buyers list – *after* Rosalind Gardner has been credited with her commission, so you're not stealing her thunder.

All of a sudden – by **writing one letter** and **having your sales material and affiliate program professionally in place** – you've got serious traffic!

Serious traffic creates significant passive income.

And each one of those buyers – who will love your well-produced information product as much as Rosalind Gardner did – has the option of **signing up to be your affiliate**. And since they themselves have affiliates, you're now looking at **tiered** affiliate sales – where you pick up more and more affiliates indirectly, which means more and more sales. And that means ever-multiplying, true **passive income**.

But wait! You've planned for and added **a Resale Rights upsell,** giving your affiliates the chance to **rebrand** your product with their own picture, name and information! Not only are you making money from their affiliate sales, you're making money from your upsells.

On top of that, you had an **OTO** (one time offer) ready and waiting as purchasers were about to check out with their purchase. 10% of your purchasers added that OTO to their carts!

Or you offered the option to add a physical version of the product for an extra fee.

And all this came about through having a plan made carefully in advance; then making the most of material you've created.

Marketer B, on the other hand, just promoted her $497 12-CD Instruction course to her 94 subscribers. She didn't have an affiliate program in place. She used just a couple of methods of promotion.

Nobody bought it.

INFORMATION PRODUCT PASSIVE INCOME

What we were just talking about was a **practical** lesson in using your business savvy to create passive income. It's what separates Mary Dabbler from Mary Entrepreneur.

Mary Dabbler downloads dozens of eBooks telling her how to market – but she doesn't really read them. She gets about one third of the way in, and gets **distracted** (triggered by a sentence or link in the eBook itself). She's off to check out some other aspect of marketing she **feels compelled to learn**. Finally, having spent more money and time than she ever intended, she somehow manages to create an information product. She's so exhausted by then, she just pushes it to her tiny list. Since she started off with a high ticket item, instead of building her list with lower ticket items or making sure she and her product gained maximum exposure and buzz first, she's disappointed when her product release is met with… **resounding silence**.

Compare that with yours – market exposure and social proof (provided by your super affiliate JV); a huge increase in your list; a product that lives up to your intelligent creation efforts (wow, only 2 returns out of 120 sales!) – and you made $5,000 with that first release!

Your return on your investment (ROI) was <u>huge</u>, for a newer marketer!

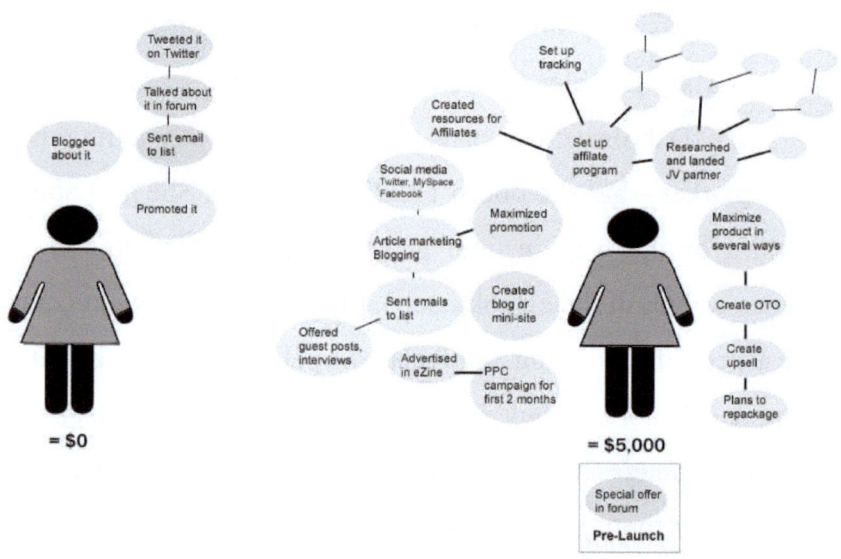

You can see from my diagram, above, that the amount of sales is almost *directly proportionate to the amount of planning and work at set up.*

But that's the beauty of **passive income with information products**: Once you've got them set up and properly launched, your product's high visibility (and that **army of affiliates**!) will keep generating income for a very long time.

You want to make that product keep on working for you, bringing in *real passive income* over the longest term possible.

Exactly how do you do that?

Add one more factor: Make it **evergreen** – a product that will be as relevant and useful ten years from now as it is today.

And *keep the buzz flowing*. **Repackage** your product in a different media, when it really starts to flag. **Repurpose** it, if you like – take your eBook, and turn it into a paid self-study course – and get *even more mileage* out of it!

Every now and then, send out a solo mailing to your list. Promote your product when you see that a long enough interval has elapsed to allow those who didn't buy the first time to consider it now. Promote it to new subscribers. Promote it when it's timely again and people are buzzing about your niche subject, or there's been a big furor about a similar product that's been released and failed dismally, giving you the perfect opportunity to create another buzz about yours. Offer yourself for guest posts or interviews.

But make no mistake: Your super affiliate's review andher shrewd marketing practices - as well as all your new affiliates, and their affiliates, etc. – are going to keep **information product passive income** coming in for a long time.

TRAPS TO AVOID

We spoke about Mary Dabbler – and if we're honest, most of us have been in her shoes. We've made several (if not all) of the mistakes she made.

We didn't make them because we were stupid: On the contrary, we made them because we were burning to learn as much as we could, and take our place with market leaders. We wanted to create real passive income and give our families security.

But with so many skilled marketers using every trick in the book to tap into our needs and fears - face it: We got played like little violins.

There's a Canadian TV show, " *Canada's Worst Driver"* – and the participants (nominated by exasperated friends and family) really are atrocious drivers.

They don't think they are. They think they're functioning well. And one of the biggest mistakes they all consistently make… these participants all consistently *take their eyes off the road and stop looking where they want to go.*

They're easily distracted.

And with the information overload we're constantly bombarded with, we are too.

Here are some hints on how to stay focused:

- **Unsubscribe** to every marketer except your relevant top 3-5 favorites

- **Learn only what you need to know** to accomplish the next task. Forget about the multitude of "must-have" special offers for now (that „disappearing' special offer will most likely be there when you finally need it. And if the price has gone up, you still saved more money in the long run by staying focused, ignoring the offer and thoroughly **learning and setting up only what you needed to**)

- **Get a coach** – especially if you feel you're *spinning your wheels*, you're *stuck at one step*, or *you've lost focus*. You don't have to sign up for some fancy-schmancy, over-hyped coaching program where you fly to the Bahamas to eat stale cookies and sip fruit drinks, pay a fortune and (after a 3-day unrelenting sales pitch) commit yourself to $5000 a year for 10 years. You can hire different coaches at different stages, for different needs. You can have just a one-time session on one particular issue, or you can commit to a monthly fee that is in line with your budget.

If your budget is really tight, sometimes joining a mastermind group is a better option for you, if you need constant input.

When you can afford it, upgrade to the "coaching" level.

But whatever you do, at least get yourself a mentor – someone who's a little ahead of you; someone who is kind enough to interest themselves in your progress; someone you can learn from.

And one other valuable asset you gain from hooking up with a coach or mentor: you're more likely to feel **accountable**, and not fritter away the day browsing interesting websites. You've got someone to report to, who's expecting a certain degree of progress made. (Though the biggest value of having a coach for me was… when you verbalize what you're doing and why, you often catch your own lame excuses! Or you see your mistakes before they even have to point them out to you!)

PASSIVE INCOME METHODS AND MEANS

Now let's look at the various methods and means of passive income generation you can pick and choose from as your source of income. We've talked about information products: Let's dig a little deeper, and see what else we have at our disposal…

Super Affiliate Marketer

Here's an idea for you… once you've built up your list with your holy- Wow **passive income product**, you can concentrate on becoming a **super affiliate** yourself.

You'll quickly see why that first super affiliate you approached is interested in **higher-ticket items**, when considering JV's – but you'll also see that, first and foremost, she was concerned with **what would please and excite her list**.

Being a super affiliate is like any other job: You need to "practice" and stick with it until what is at first a struggle becomes an easy, familiar routine. (And – like any other 9-5 job you've worked at – it *will* become easy and familiar, if you just stick with it, and don't give up.)

On your way to being a super affiliate, you really can be making significant sums of income – perhaps even duplicating your monthly salary in a week – or a day – once your affiliate ball is rolling smoothly.

Driving Traffic to your Products

How you drive traffic to your products will differ – and make a big difference to how much passive income those products bring in. Some top affiliate marketers never touch paid advertising, for example; others swear by it – even if they do it just long enough to kick-start new campaigns.

PPC – Pay Per Click ads are both a blessing and a curse. Why?

Because you can't control how many people are going to click on your ad and actually visit your link to subscribe.

You can't even control how many people are just going to click on your ad.

If lots subscribe, and several buy, it might be well worth the cost of the ads – but if *everyone clicks and no one buys* – that's a new marketer's worst nightmare.

You're paying for every single one of those clicks!

Fortunately, with most PPC networks, you can **set a daily limit**, and **bid on lower-cost keywords** that have enough traffic to be viable but not enough to be nose-bleedingly expensive per click.

You can also terminate the campaign, once the ball has started rolling and sales are coming in at a decent rate. Or you can keep it going, if you've determined – through **tracking** – that your PPC ads are a major factor in those good monthly profits.

Keyword Research

I said we'd get back to this later on, and this seems like the perfect time to go into more detail.

It's a given that knowing how to do effective keyword research is one of the basics you should master straight away. So how do the gurus and super affiliates do their keyword research?

While it's true that many do have favorite paid products they like such as Traffic Travis, Market Samurai and

MicroNicheFinder, you'd be surprised how many super affiliates don't bother with paid programs, but keep their keyword research simple.

One reason: they have focused so much on the lists they serve, they've developed a strong, natural feel for what's going to work and what is not. They've got an ear on the „net, and they know what trends are hot, what's evergreen, what problems their niche members are having … their keyword research, and the long-tailed keywords they pick, are informed by all these factors.

But they do actually still research keywords, and here are two of the most popular methods I've seen used by super affiliates…

Method # 1

1. Access Wordtracker's freekeywords tool and type in your keyword. Pick likely long-tailed keywords (3 words or more) from the results.

2. Check these phrases in Google's search box, contained in quotes.

3. If there are a good number of searches, but these searches are still under 150,000, you've most likely got a viable niche to work

Method # 2

This just takes the above method one step further…

1. Access Wordtracker and find some long-tailed keywords you think might be likely suspects

2. Go to <u>Google Adwords KeyTool</u> (it's free) and enter your phrases

3. Check the results (use "exact" mode, and focus only on monthly global search.)

4. If the results for your phrase show some keyword competition (the little green "bars" are present and your results are over 1,000 in exact monthly global search, go to Google.

5. Check the phrase, in quotes, in their search box. If your results in Google Search still fit the under-150,000 criteria, you've got a winner!

The **lower** the number **in Google**, the better – but it should still have a good number of searches.

The **higher in Adwords**, the better – but there's a point where Adwords competition is too strong.

Use your common sense to decide what will work for you.)

How Do You Find Them?

You've got a great keyword, and a great niche (and this applies whether you're planning to create an info product or strictly stick to affiliate marketing other people's products.) Now… how do you find your market?

If you've come to these keywords as the tail end of a journey that started with a huge buzz in a market you're already familiar with, and your great keywords are merely confirmation of that, you've got the problem solved.

But if (as often happens, when searching for something else) you've come across your wonderful niche and phrase by accident, you may actually need to physically "find" your market.

This job will be made easier, once you realize they're as much a community as the church you go to, or the equestrian group you're associated with.

If you're a 3-day eventer, you'll already know all the local major equestrian centers in your state or province who have facilities set up for 3-day eventing. You keep an eye on upcoming events, and either enter you and your horse, or go as a spectator.

You know what magazines to buy regularly, to find out this news. You know what newsletters to subscribe to – and what association websites to watch.

If you're completely outside your new niche, you may not organically know that you ought to be keeping an eye on Grandview Farm's website for upcoming event listings. So you need to do a bit of scouting.

Where do you find out where you need to go?

On the net, a good start is to enter your keyword phrase in Google search, and see, first of all, if there are any trade or non-profit or governing associations for your niche. These are often good places to start, when looking to glean clues about where to go and "hang out", and what to join.

Another technique you should practice: Enter your keyword phrase in Google (in quotes) and add (without my quotes, here) **"+ forum"**.

Visit these forums. See which forums have larger numbers, and which ones are **active.** This is very important, since you don't want to waste your efforts on a forum that always has the same 3 posters!

If a forum meets your criteria, enter your keyword phrase into their search box (without quotes) – and monitor the posts for a good while, before you actually make contact.

You can also look for hashtags and lists on Twitter. I find Twitter is a great source, when I need to discover more about a particular niche.

Talking to your Niche

How do you get attention from your niche? More to the point, how do you get them to click on your sales or affiliate links?

We've already discussed the biggest essentials:

- Make it all about them

- Hang out on social media or forums where they do – and be the "solver", whenever someone's got a problem

- Empathize with them, and get to know them. Be interested in their interests, and help them with their problems

But there's one more subject we haven't touched: Your blog set up and design.

If you're an affiliate marketer, you're going to have several blogs, landing pages and mini-sites set up. Here are some of the essentials to watch out for:

Blogs – *design*. As super affiliate Lynn Terry says, people have become "banner blind" to sidebar ads and banner ads. She keeps her sidebars clear, reminds us that people start reading in the top left corner of the actual content section – and stop when they come to the end. *They don't go back up to find your affiliate link*, even if they've thoroughly enjoyed your post.

That's why it's especially important to **always leave your readers with a definite call to action** at the end of your post.

Another thing to remember – if you do have ads and links that you want your readers to click on, make your colors match and blend. Don't use ads or link colors that stick out like a sore thumb – readers' tastes have become more sophisticated since the days when flashing banners were a holy-Wow novelty. In-your-face graphics, borders, backgrounds and colors are a big turn-off.

Blogs – *content*. While it's true you really want to entertain, help or otherwise provide great content for your readers, never lose sight that each post should promote a product or service – in other words, you want them to take that call to action and **click on your link**.

In offline retail terms… you want to **close that sale**. Reviews are a powerful way to do this. The reason?

When people want to check out a product or find a product, the word "review" is usually part of their search input.

By reviewing a product, you're providing a service for them. Telling them the cons, as well as the pros, helps keep it real and makes you seem more credible.

They're already pre-qualified and partially pre-sold by their interest in the subject you're blogging about. Help them out one step further by telling them where they can buy the product you've just used – finish with a call to action to click on the link. ("You can purchase the complete package at Amazon.com"…)

It's very important that, while you want to be known as the problem solver and expert, you absolutely do *not* want to give the impression that you've positioned yourself "above" them in your own mind. Don't be so impersonal that you come off like a minor deity – someone they can't relate to.

Don't pour out your most intimate personal details and problems either, of course – but do let them see you're a human being, and that the problems they face are ones you've experienced too.

Remember to include those intriguing, irresistible, empathy-loaded headlines… preferably with well-optimized keywords included, if you can manage it. (If you do this, place the long-tailed keyword in your first sentence too, if it doesn't sound forced.)

And don't forget the legal stuff, like disclosures and disclaimers! (The FTC's new rules are set to start, December 1, 2009!)

And last, but definitely not least – I'm sure you know what I'm going to say, by now – that **call to action**!

So… we've covered a lot. What is left?

Well, that leaves us to sneak a peek at our last passive income tool…

CPA Marketing

CPA, or cost-per-action marketing, is something you can add to your blogs – or get into, for its own sake.

The great thing about Cost Per Action is the "action" part: You get paid if people merely click on the link provided, because these links are strictly for lead generation.

Unless you know how to maximize CPA, however, you can end up putting a lot of work into something that brings you a downright piddly return. Here's what you need to know:

- Some niches bring in significantly higher rewards, because they're funded by markets with huge budgets

- Some CPA networks are better than others
- Some CPA offers allow you not only to get paid for lead generation, but will *pay commissions on actual sales, too* – so it's worth your time to put a little more energy into promoting them.
- Some CPA networks also reward you for good sales. These are ones you'll be especially interested in, as a super affiliate.

Pepperjam and ShareaSale are two of the more popular CPA networks. And here are a few more, for you to check out as you get a feel for CPA marketing…

AZN Network
Directleads
Eadvertising
Hydra
Incentaclick
Neverblueads
Offerweb
Trafficneeds

WHY YOU NEED TO TRACK

We haven't said too much about this, because it's a natural part of becoming an internet marketer you have to learn anyway – even if all you're doing is tracking your Tweet stats, using Google Analytics and checking which pages bring traffic in your cPanel via your FTP program.

If you're not tracking, you won't maximize your income potential: It's as simple as that.

You need to know:

- Which squeeze pages work, and which don't Which headlines work – and which work better
- Whether your long sales letter or short one gives you a higher conversion rate
- Where you are losing people throughout your sales funnel, if you're marketing your own product

- If your product's shopping cart pages has any "bounce" points – where potential customers encounter a "glitch", get frustrated, and leave

All this, you learn through vigilant tracking and testing.

Even more crucially, there are **glitches that can happen with product sellers' systems**, causing you to **lose credit on affiliate sales you've driven there**. Be vigilant, because this can occur any time – even when you've been happily receiving regular affiliate commission cheques from a particular marketer for years.

Most people whose products you promote are quick to fix these glitches and credit you for sales, when you point out the down time – especially if you're one of their top affiliates. But sadly, there are others who are not so scrupulous – and these are not necessarily "small potato" product owners, either. There was a case, recently, where two of the top affiliate marketers angrily denounced a top industry software company for quietly changing their policies and cheating these two particular super affiliates out of well-deserved – and major – amounts of commission.

(Shockingly, when I last checked into this, the software company had still not rectified this, and seemed to be ignoring the issue!)

We would all rather believe that everyone has the high standards we do, but the truth is, you really do have to track your sales and commissions. You can't assume that everyone up in the top layers of the stratosphere there is honorable. (And mistakes and technical glitches do occur.)

If you'd like to investigate tracking tools further, Prosper202 is free. Statsrobot is also a program with a good reputation.

I hope this special report has given you what you need, to start deciding on your best way to create passive income – but whatever method you use… whether you're happy adding $14 of Adsense and the odd $30 from Amazon to your marketing efforts or you've decided to go whole-hog on the Super Affiliate path, with your own passive - income generating products and a healthy dose of highly-converting insurance and mortgage CPA on the side – do seriously consider adding passive income to your marketing plan.

Now git out there and start racking up that powerful "word of mouth" credibility – and let me hear that buzz!

Printed by Libri Plureos GmbH in Hamburg,
Germany